STEVE IRWIN

A Little Golden Book® Biography

AF751623

By Sarah Mahoney

Illustrated by Caroline Garcia

A GOLDEN BOOK

Penguin Random House Australia is part of the Penguin Random House group
of companies whose addresses can be found at global.penguinrandomhouse.com.
First published by Penguin Books, an imprint of Penguin Random House Australia Pty Ltd, in 2026
Copyright © Penguin Random House Australia Pty Ltd
Illustrations copyright © Caroline Garcia 2026
Design by Rebecca King © Penguin Random House Australia Pty Ltd
The moral right of the author and illustrator has been asserted.
All rights reserved. No part of this publication may be reproduced, published,
performed in public or communicated to the public in any form or by any means
without prior written permission from Penguin Random House Australia Pty Ltd,
Penguin Random House LLC or its authorised licensees.
Golden Books, A Golden Book, A Little Golden Book, the G colophon,
and the distinctive gold spine are registered trademarks of Penguin Random House LLC.
Printed and bound in China
A catalogue record for this book is available from the National Library of Australia
ISBN 9781761358845(Hardback)

HAPPY BIRTHDAY

Steve Robert Irwin was born on 22 February 1962 in Upper Ferntree Gully, Victoria, Australia. He had two sisters and shared his birthday with his mum, Lyn.

Both Steve's parents loved animals. His dad, Bob, liked to study reptiles and Steve's mum took care of sick and injured wallabies.

When Steve was eight, his family moved to Beerwah, Queensland, where they built their own reptile and native animal park. Steve loved having a zoo for a backyard! He explored the park and learned about all the animals that came into his family's care.

He was especially fascinated by reptiles, including snakes and crocodiles. So, when Steve wasn't helping his mum and sisters look after baby animals, he went on adventures with his dad to move crocodiles to safer waterways. His dad taught him how to respect crocodiles and to handle them safely.

Steve was brave and, by the time he was nine, he was already jumping on the backs of smaller crocodiles and wrestling them into his dad's dinghy!

As he grew older, he
became a crocodile expert.
It was his favourite animal.

At home in the park, Steve enjoyed showing off the crocodile's power and beauty.

Curious onlookers would watch as Steve climbed into an enclosure and held food for them to snatch out of his hands. His crocodile shows were a huge hit!

The park was also home to lots of other animals, including kangaroos, wombats, koalas and birds. After Steve took over managing the park in 1991, he wanted to find other ways to help protect wildlife. He hoped that by sharing his love for animals, everyone would want to help protect them, too.

One day, Steve's life changed forever when he met Terri Raines, who was visiting from America. It was love at first sight.

Terri shared Steve's love for wildlife. They made a great team.

After Steve and Terri got married, they invited a film crew to tag along on what sounded like an unusual honeymoon – a crocodile rescue mission!

The footage from that trip was made into a pilot episode for a new TV show called *The Crocodile Hunter*.

The show aired in 1996, and Steve quickly became a TV star. Millions of people watched him fearlessly wrestle crocs and handle venomous snakes.

His excitement about animals won him lots of fans and his catchphrase 'Crikey!' became world-famous. Most importantly, when Steve talked about wildlife conservation, people listened.

Some people thought Steve was being reckless, but he knew that his close encounters with animals made people pay attention. He was raising awareness and appreciation for endangered animals and bringing the natural world right into people's living rooms.

With each season of *The Crocodile Hunter*, more people visited the park. Steve and Terri renamed it Australia Zoo and worked hard to make it bigger and better. They even built a 'crocoseum' – an arena where they could put on Steve's amazing crocodile shows for thousands of people!

For Steve and Terri, the animals always came first. The couple put the money they made from the TV show and the zoo back into animal conservation.

In 2004, Australia Zoo opened its very own animal hospital, in memory of Steve's mum, who passed away four years prior. What started out as an old avocado shed on his parents' land became one of the biggest and busiest wildlife hospitals in the world.

Steve and Terri also started a charity that supports other programs around the world that care for and protect endangered animals.

Sadly, Steve passed away in 2006. But his love for animals lives on through his children, Bindi and Robert, who work with their mum at Australia Zoo. Together, they continue Steve's mission to inspire new generations and to teach them about animals and wildlife conservation.

Anyone can make a big difference in the world. Like Steve, all you need is passion, bravery and a single dream.